READY SET GROW

IDENTITY

*The Search That
Leads to Significance
and True Success*

STUDY GUIDE

Copyright © 2022 by Scott Wilson

Published by AVAIL

All rights reserved. No portion of this book may be reproduced, stored in a retrieval system, or transmitted in any form or by any means—electronic, mechanical, photocopy, recording, scanning, or other—except for brief quotations in critical reviews or articles, without prior written permission of the author.

Scripture quotations marked NIV are taken from the Holy Bible, New International Version®, NIV®. Copyright © 1973, 1978, 1984, 2011 by Biblica, Inc.™ Used by permission of Zondervan. All rights reserved worldwide. www.zondervan.com. The "NIV" and "New International Version" are trademarks registered in the United States Patent and Trademark Office by Biblica, Inc.™

For foreign and subsidiary rights, contact the author.

Cover design by Joe De Leon
Cover Photo by Andrew van Tilborgh

ISBN: 978-1-957369-03-7   1 2 3 4 5 6 7 8 9 10

Printed in the United States of America

— READY SET GROW —

IDENTITY

*The Search That
Leads to Significance
and True Success*

STUDY GUIDE

S C O T T
W I L S O N

CONTENTS

Introduction Lifting the Lid 6

CHAPTER 1. The Dream 10

CHAPTER 2. Crushed and Rebuilt... 14

CHAPTER 3. Breaking the Orphan Mindset 20

CHAPTER 4. Self-Sabotage 26

CHAPTER 5. God Picked Me.. 32

CHAPTER 6. A Gift from God.. 36

CHAPTER 7. Cutting Ties 40

CHAPTER 8. Growing Up, Stepping Out 46

CHAPTER 9. A Higher Calling... 50

INTRODUCTION

LIFTING THE LID

God has given you a new, revolutionary identity, as well as the skills, gifts, and talents to fulfill the purpose He put in your heart.

As you read the Introduction: "Lifting the Lid" in *Identity: The Search That Leads to Significance and True Success*, review, reflect on, and respond to the text by answering the following questions.

REVIEW, REFLECT, AND RESPOND:

What are some things that the grace of God accomplishes?

_____
_____
_____
_____
_____
_____

How has pursuing God's purpose for your life impacted yourself and those around you?

_____
_____
_____
_____
_____
_____

Recall some of the voices from your past that may have caused you to second guess your purpose. Have you been able to overcome those negative voices?

_____
_____
_____
_____
_____
_____

Describe a scenario in which you've relied on your performance as a means of finding significance. How did this affect you when you were performing well? Poorly?

_____
_____
_____
_____
_____
_____
_____

Have you had spiritual fathers or mothers speak into your life? Who were/are they? How did God use them in your life?

_____
_____
_____
_____
_____
_____
_____

What doubts do you have about being used by God?

_____
_____
_____
_____
_____
_____
_____

> *What no eye has seen, what no ear has heard, and what no human mind has conceived—the things God has prepared for those who love him—these are the things God has revealed to us by his Spirit.*
>
> *—1 Corinthians 2:9-10*

Consider the scripture above and answer the following questions:

How does this scripture relate to discovering your identity in Christ?

_____
_____
_____
_____
_____
_____
_____
_____
_____
_____

In what ways has the Holy Spirit revealed this truth to you?

_____
_____
_____
_____
_____
_____
_____

CHAPTER 1

THE DREAM

My dad poured himself into me, and he believed in me when there was no visible reason to have that level of confidence in me. That's what good dads do. They see you, not for who you are, but for the person you are becoming. And they call that greatness out in you.

As you read Chapter 1: "The Dream" in *Identity: The Search That Leads to Significance and True Success*, review, reflect on, and respond to the text by answering the following questions.

REVIEW, REFLECT, AND RESPOND:

Have you ever had a person who believed in you more than you believed in yourself? How did their involvement in your life produce positive results?

_____
_____
_____
_____
_____
_____

Describe a time when you felt that God was "holding out" on you. How did you emerge from that time period?

_____
_____
_____
_____
_____
_____

How does comparison to others inhibit the process God has for your life?

_____
_____
_____
_____
_____
_____

Has God ever revealed Himself to you in a similar way as He did with Scott's dream? Share that experience and revelation.

_____
_____
_____
_____

On whose shoulders are *you* standing? Who paved the way for you?

_____
_____
_____
_____

How did their choices allow you to stand on their work to do greater things?

_____
_____
_____
_____

Are you posturing yourself to allow another to stand on *your* shoulders? How so?

_____
_____
_____
_____

What can you be doing right now to intentionally develop the next generation (no matter your age) to stand on your shoulders?

_____
_____
_____
_____

> *Very truly I tell you, whoever believes in me will do the works I have been doing, and they will do even greater things than these, because I am going to the Father. And I will do whatever you ask in my name, so that the Father may be glorified in the Son. You may ask me for anything in my name, and I will do it.*
>
> *—John 14:12-14*

Consider the scripture above and answer the following questions:

What do you experience when you stand on the shoulders of Jesus?

_____
_____
_____
_____

Explain the importance of glorifying God as you "do greater things."

_____
_____
_____
_____

CHAPTER 2

CRUSHED AND REBUILT

My heavenly Father broke through my despair and my shattered dreams to say, "You need to trust in My plan. You need to trust in My timing. I'm the Lord. Do you think I'm going to delegate the responsibility to shape you to John? Trust Me even when your hopes are dashed. Trust Me when you're disappointed, when you go through hard times, when things aren't moving as fast as you'd like. Trust Me like Jesus trusted Me."

As you read Chapter 2: "Crushed and Rebuilt" in *Identity: The Search That Leads to Significance and True Success*, review, reflect on, and respond to the text by answering the following questions.

REVIEW, REFLECT, AND RESPOND:

Share your story of a shattered dream.

_____
_____
_____
_____
_____
_____
_____
_____
_____
_____
_____

Have you ever set yourself up in your mind or plans (like Scott did in his meeting with John) for something great only to be let down by reality? What did that look like for you?

_____
_____
_____
_____
_____
_____
_____

Has there ever been a time that you looked to another leader as your "source"? Did you realize it at the time?

_____
_____
_____
_____
_____
_____
_____

What was the result of putting God in second chair?

_____
_____
_____
_____
_____
_____

Has God ever used a leader to guide and mentor you from afar? Who was/is that?

_____
_____
_____
_____
_____
_____
_____

Describe a time when you were attempting to control an outcome instead of trusting God's timing. How did you emerge from that?

_____
_____
_____
_____
_____
_____
_____
_____

Why do you think God's path includes darkness, heartache, and setbacks?

_____
_____
_____
_____
_____
_____
_____
_____

Have you ever gone through a painful season of reorientation? How did God use your pain to help you grow?

_____
_____
_____
_____
_____
_____
_____

> *It was just before the Passover Festival. Jesus knew that the hour had come for him to leave this world and go to the Father. Having loved his own who were in the world, he loved them to the end*
>
> —*John 13:1*

Consider the scripture above and answer the following questions:

What do you think John meant when he said that Jesus "loved them to the end?" Do you agree with Scott's assessment here?

_____
_____
_____
_____
_____
_____
_____
_____
_____
_____

How do you love someone to the *nth* degree?

_____
_____
_____
_____
_____
_____
_____
_____
_____
_____

CHAPTER 3

BREAKING THE ORPHAN MINDSET

Those who walk closely with God have a beautiful blend of zeal and contentment. Their drive isn't clouded by comparison or the fear of not measuring up. They can give it all they've got and trust that God will do what only He can do.

As you read Chapter 3: "Breaking the Orphan Mindset" in *Identity: The Search That Leads to Significance and True Success*, review, reflect on, and respond to the text by answering the following questions.

REVIEW, REFLECT, AND RESPOND:

Describe a time in which you tried to "push and shove" to make something happen. How did that turn out for you?

_____
_____
_____
_____
_____
_____
_____
_____
_____
_____
_____

How did you reverse that method and begin to trust that God would make a way for you?

_____
_____
_____
_____
_____
_____
_____
_____
_____
_____

Consider Scott's statement: *"I discovered that contentment is the byproduct of certainty."* What does this mean to you?

_____
_____
_____
_____
_____

How does one live in a state of contentment?

_____
_____
_____
_____

What sort of fears or insecurities may result from having an "orphan mindset"?

_____
_____
_____
_____

How does having an "orphan mindset" manifest in ministry?

_____
_____
_____
_____

Do you see signs of this mindset in yourself? In others? What does that look like?

_____

_____

_____

_____

_____

_____

_____

_____

_____

What does it mean to be God-made versus self-made?

_____

_____

_____

_____

> *Jesus said to them, "You will indeed drink from my cup..."*
> —*Matthew 20:23*

Consider the scripture above and answer the following questions:

What did Jesus mean by "drink from my cup?"

_____
_____
_____
_____
_____
_____
_____
_____
_____

Do you think James and John understood what Jesus meant by that?

_____
_____
_____
_____
_____
_____
_____
_____
_____

CHAPTER 4

SELF-SABOTAGE

I could trust him and take steps forward, or I could walk away from his input into my life. We might continue to meet, but it would never be the same. I took a deep breath and announced, "It's really hard for me to get my head around it, but I'll listen to you, and I'll do what you say."

As you read Chapter 4: "Self-Sabotage" in *Identity: The Search That Leads to Significance and True Success*, review, reflect on, and respond to the text by answering the following questions.

REVIEW, REFLECT, AND RESPOND:

Do you have mentors, coaches, counselors, or consultants speaking into your life? Who are they?

_____
_____
_____
_____
_____
_____

Describe a time when one of these people spoke plainly and directly into your situation and you were resistant to their wisdom. Did you recognize the need to listen or ignore their advice?

_____
_____
_____
_____
_____
_____
_____
_____
_____
_____
_____

Why would skepticism inhibit a person's ability to help others?

How does having a poverty mindset stifle growth?

When a leader models the way to seek Christ and make commitments, that inspires those they lead. How can you model your commitment?

Why would Sam ask Scott to model his need for a miracle?

Share your story of modeling that led to miracles and breakthroughs.

_____
_____
_____
_____

Have you carried a weight that you were not intended to carry? How did you release that weight?

_____
_____
_____
_____
_____

What are some "spots" that you need to address? Who can help you?

_____
_____
_____
_____
_____

> *Let the wise listen and add to their learning,*
> *and let the discerning get guidance.*
>
> *—Proverbs 1:5*

Consider the scripture above and answer the following questions:

Why are we, as Christians, instructed to seek wise counsel and guidance?

_____
_____
_____
_____
_____
_____
_____
_____
_____

What does the Bible say about those who disregard wise input?

_____
_____
_____
_____
_____
_____
_____
_____
_____

CHAPTER 5

GOD PICKED ME

One of the biggest errors in the church world is the assumption that full-time Christian workers are "called by God," and everybody else is just filling seats and giving money for pastors, staff, and missionaries to do God's work. Thankfully, that misconception has been shattered in most churches, but I'm not sure we've done a good enough job communicating the order of calling to everybody in the church.

As you read Chapter 5: "God Picked Me" in *Identity: The Search That Leads to Significance and True Success*, review, reflect on, and respond to the text by answering the following questions.

REVIEW, REFLECT, AND RESPOND:

What have been your observations or experience with succession?

_____
_____
_____
_____
_____
_____
_____
_____
_____
_____

Why would money, identity, and marriage be the three largest factors that affect the path of succession planning?

_____
_____
_____
_____
_____
_____
_____
_____
_____
_____
_____

Scott describes setbacks, delays, and disagreements as threats to his identity and role as Lead Pastor in the days, even years, after assuming that position. How does his experience resonate with you?

_____
_____
_____
_____

What would be the value of engaging help from someone who has already walked this path?

_____
_____
_____
_____

Describe the tension between how you feel when things are going well versus when things are not going well.

_____
_____
_____
_____

Consider this statement: *"We react by running around to fix things to make people happy with us."* What is the danger of doing this?

_____
_____
_____
_____

Why does Scott refer to one's performance as a cruel master?

_____
_____
_____

How does having God at the center of our cause allow us to extend kindness and care to all?

_____
_____
_____
_____
_____

> *Dear friends, now we are children of God, and what we will be has not yet been made known. But we know that when Christ appears, we shall be like him, for we shall see him as he is. All who have this hope in him purify themselves, just as he is pure.*
>
> *—John 3:2-3*

Consider the scripture above and answer the following questions:

Why should Christians take comfort in knowing that we are children of God, even if life doesn't go the way we want it to?

_____
_____
_____
_____
_____

How should we respond to the cause of God? Does this look different or the same for everyone?

_____
_____
_____
_____
_____

CHAPTER 6

A GIFT FROM GOD

Investing in others is the heartbeat of God. That's the message of the gospel: God invested His Son in saving those who didn't deserve it, and He continues to invest Himself in those who trust in Him. We gain by giving away. We rise by stooping to serve. We plant seeds of love, so other people can grow strong.

As you read Chapter 6: "A Gift from God" in *Identity: The Search That Leads to Significance and True Success*, review, reflect on, and respond to the text by answering the following questions.

REVIEW, REFLECT, AND RESPOND:

Have you ever been given an unexpected opportunity that you later realized was organized by God?

_____
_____
_____
_____
_____
_____
_____
_____

Describe the moment you knew it was God-orchestrated and what that meant to your life.

_____
_____
_____
_____
_____
_____
_____
_____
_____
_____
_____
_____
_____

Was that opportunity a dream deferred like Scott's? Reconcile the "old you" with the "new you" who received that opportunity.

_____
_____
_____
_____

Make a list of the differences in yourself from one time period to the next.

_____
_____
_____
_____

What does it reveal about a person when they can enjoy an accolade without idolizing it?

_____
_____
_____
_____

What do you think Scott means when he says that young people need to have their motives tempered? What has that looked like for you?

_____
_____
_____
_____

Consider the shift Joseph made from his dream being about himself to it being about how he can save and serve his family. What dreams of yours have shifted with time, tests, and revelations?

_____
_____

How did the manifestation of those dreams assist those around you, in other generations?

> *All of you, clothe yourselves with humility toward one another, because, "God opposes the proud but shows favor to the humble." Humble yourselves, therefore, under God's mighty hand, that he may lift you up in due time. Cast all your anxiety on him because he cares for you.*
>
> —*1 Peter 5:5-7*

Consider the scripture above and answer the following questions:

How is this verse in opposition to the way the world operates?

Why is God opposed to self-promotion or seeking to control?

CHAPTER 7

CUTTING TIES

It appears that God has kept me in "school" majoring in the same subject for the entirety of my life. . . . God's course load is about grasping the wonder that the infinitely powerful God is also infinitely loving . . . toward me! I'm a child of the King, deeply loved, completely forgiven, and totally accepted—not because of my performance, but apart from it—or more accurately, in spite of it. It's all about grace. As my heavenly Father, He knows what's best for me, He knows the right path for me, He knows the right timing for me . . . so I can relax and trust Him.

As you read Chapter 7: "Cutting Ties" in *Identity: The Search That Leads to Significance and True Success*, review, reflect on, and respond to the text by answering the following questions.

REVIEW, REFLECT, AND RESPOND:

Have you ever had to cut ties with people in your life who were of great resource to you (maybe they were of greater resource to you than God)?

_____
_____
_____
_____
_____
_____
_____
_____
_____

How did you recognize their "over significance" in your life? How did you release them honorably?

_____
_____
_____
_____
_____
_____
_____
_____
_____
_____

Do you currently depend on any one person more than you depend on God? Ask Him to reveal that barrier between Him and yourself, if so.

Has God ever said, "Just do it!" to you? What was He asking you to do? Did you obey?

How has God purged you of your doubts and hesitations in the past?

Why do you think it is so difficult for some to release control and fully depend on God?

_____

_____

_____

_____

Reflect on how this statement applies to your life: "His calling preceded my preparation, and my obedience preceded God's revelation of the exact nature of the calling."

_____

_____

_____

_____

What are some boundaries that you need to set up for yourself so that you can remain open to receiving wisdom directly from God?

_____

_____

_____

_____

_____

> *Wounds from a friend can be trusted...*
> —*Proverbs 27:6*

Consider the scripture above and answer the following questions:

How can wounds from a friend be unsettling?

_____
_____
_____
_____

Describe a situation in which you were wounded by a friend and how their challenge was of help to you.

_____
_____
_____
_____
_____
_____
_____
_____
_____
_____
_____

CHAPTER 8

GROWING UP, STEPPING OUT

If you're a teacher, a coach, an aunt or uncle, a grandparent, or a team leader in any organization, you have the unspeakable privilege of speaking truth into the lives of those around you. God has put you there for a reason. It's no mistake, and God will use you to see potential others have missed, to heal hurts, to provide support, and to help them take the next steps on the path God has opened to them.

As you read Chapter 8: "Growing Up, Stepping Out" in *Identity: The Search That Leads to Significance and True Success*, review, reflect on, and respond to the text by answering the following questions.

REVIEW, REFLECT, AND RESPOND:

Why is a person's self-image the limiting factor for growth?

_____
_____
_____
_____
_____
_____
_____
_____
_____

How does David's story of relational trauma highlight the fact that healing from such pain is an every day decision?

_____
_____
_____
_____
_____
_____
_____
_____
_____
_____
_____

What situation from your life most closely resembles David's in which you had to make a decision to soften your heart in the middle of a bad circumstance?

_____
_____
_____
_____

What is the value of understanding the context of the time period between David's anointing and his killing of Goliath?

_____
_____
_____
_____

Why has God chosen *you* to be great?

_____
_____
_____
_____

As a parent, why is it critical to notice greatness in your children and call it out?

_____
_____
_____
_____

Why should our identity be "gospel-shaped" for our children?

_____
_____

_____

_____

How does Scott's parallel between David's palace, where he finally recognized himself as king, and your home as a palace speak to you?

_____

_____

_____

_____

> *Now Hiram king of Tyre sent envoys to David, along with cedar logs and carpenters and stonemasons, and they built a palace for David. Then David knew that the Lord had established him as king over Israel and had exalted his kingdom for the sake of his people Israel.*
> —2 Samuel 5:11-12

Consider the scripture above and answer the following questions:

What did it take for David to change his self-image?

_____

_____

_____

_____

Describe the tension that occurs when our self-image does not match what we say we believe.

_____

_____

_____

_____

CHAPTER 9

A HIGHER CALLING

Some have wondered if I'm too young to be a spiritual father. The role isn't about age; it's about heart and calling. I've had that role since I was in my twenties. I believe it's the primary calling of every believer: to pour ourselves into others, so they excel in fulfilling whatever God puts on their hearts. There is no greater joy. My success isn't defined by what I do but by how I can help others do great things for God.

As you read Chapter 9: "A Higher Calling" in *Identity: The Search That Leads to Significance and True Success*, review, reflect on, and respond to the text by answering the following questions.

REVIEW, REFLECT, AND RESPOND:

Has God ever affirmed you via another person such as he did for Scott via John?

_____
_____
_____
_____
_____

Share that experience.

_____
_____
_____
_____
_____
_____
_____
_____
_____
_____
_____
_____
_____
_____

What are the four ways a father is formed?

1) _____
2) _____
3) _____
4) _____

Which of those four ways had the greatest impact on you as you read this chapter?

_____
_____
_____
_____

What dream has God shaped in your heart?

_____
_____
_____
_____

How can you live out a calling "under the platform"?

_____
_____
_____
_____

Who has God called you to serve "under the platform"?

_____
_____
_____
_____
_____

> *... You are my Son, whom I love; with you I am well pleased.*
> *—Luke 3:22*

Consider the scripture above and answer the following questions:

God gave Jesus this identity before He began His ministry on earth. What does that reveal to you?

_____
_____
_____
_____
_____
_____
_____
_____
_____
_____

How does this sort of love—that give an identity, affection, and affirmation—humble you?

_____
_____
_____
_____
_____
_____
_____
_____

www.ingramcontent.com/pod-product-compliance
Lightning Source LLC
Chambersburg PA
CBHW062123080426
42734CB00012B/2974